The Baking Book

Jane Bull

DK Publishing, Inc.

LONDON, NEW YORK, MUNICH,
MELBOURNE, and DELHI

DESIGN • Jane Bull
EDITOR • Penelope Arlon
PHOTOGRAPHY • Andy Crawford
DESIGNER • Sadie Thomas
DTP DESIGNER • Almudena Díaz
PRODUCTION • Alison Lenane

PUBLISHING MANAGER • Sue Leonard
MANAGING ART EDITOR • Clare Shedden

For **Baba**

First American Edition, 2005

Published in the United States by
DK Publishing, Inc.
375 Hudson Street
New York, New York 10014

05 06 07 08 09   10 9 8 7 6 5 4 3 2 1

A Cataloging-in-Publication record for this book
is available from the Library of Congress.

ISBN: 0-7566-1373-6

Color reproduction by
GRB Editrice S.r.l., Verona, Italy
Printed and bound in
Mexico by R.R. Donnelley and Sons Co.

Discover more at
www.dk.com

Bring out the chunky cookies

Bake a batch of . . .

cherry pies or clever scones . . .

. . . then whisk up a mountain

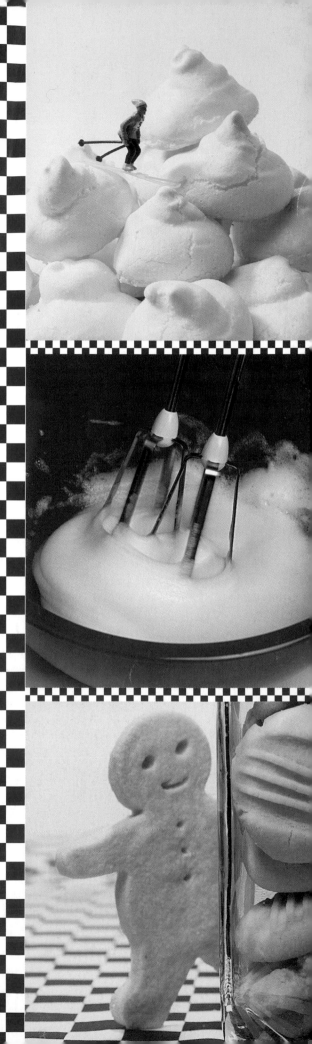

Baking basics

Getting started Here are the things you will need to bake the recipes in this book.

Safe baking

Warning! Look for this sign and be careful.

- When you see this sign, ask an adult to help you.
- An adult should always be around when you are in the kitchen.
- Ovens are HOT—wear your oven mitts.

Measure out your ingredients before you start—that way you won't leave anything out.

measuring out

REMEMBER: if you start a recipe using US customary measures, then stick to them. Don't switch to metrics partway through the recipe.

MEASURING SPOONS are very useful; they have standard sizes from tablespoons to half teaspoons.

Kitchen rules

BE PREPARED—Lay out all the ingredients and utensils that you will need for the recipe.

WASH UP—always wash your hands before you cook.

COVER UP—Wear an apron to protect your clothes.

CLEAN UP—It's your mess; you clear it up! Keep the kitchen neat as you go along. Then you can cook again!

MEASURING CUP for measuring liquids.

WEIGHING SCALES for measuring dry ingredients.

MEASURING SPOONS for measuring small amounts.

How long will it take?
The clock tells you how long to bake the recipe and will warn you to turn on the oven early to get it to the right temperature.

How much will it make?
This symbol tells you how much the recipe will make: e.g., 12 cookies or 24 mini breads.

4

your baking kit

WOODEN SPOON

COOKIE CUTTERS

SPOONS

FORK

KNIFE

PASTRY BRUSH

BAKING SHEET

ROLLING PIN

LOTS OF BOWLS

ELECTRIC MIXER

LOAF PAN

MUFFIN PAN

MIXING BOWL

BUN PAN

COOLING RACK

YOUR (CLEAN) HANDS

PARCHMENT PAPER

CAKE PANS 8 IN (20 CM)

5

cookie collection

To start you off

all you need are three things:

All-purpose flour
1¼ cups

+

Superfine sugar
¼ cup

+

Butter
1 stick (½ cup)

=

🙂 **24 cookies**
plain shortbread

Mmmm...
They look good!

1 recipe x 10

These are no ordinary cookies—with just a little pinch here and a touch of decoration there, you can make 10 completely different cookies. 10 cookies in one!

1

2

3

4

5

6

7

8

9

10

yum yum

Turn the page
to discover the
magic ingredients.

How to make shortbread cookies

Rubbing in—This is the way you mix the flour, butter, and sugar together. Rub the mixture between your thumb and fingertips until it looks like bread crumbs (see page 46).

COOKIE EQUIPMENT

MIXING BOWL

BAKING SHEET

FORK

COOLING RACK

1 In it all goes

Put all the ingredients into the bowl.

Sugar

Flour

Butter

2 Rub it together

Rub the mixture between your thumbs and fingertips.

Add flavorings

3 Make a ball

When the mixture looks crumbly, squeeze it together to make a ball of dough.

4 Roll little balls

Pinch off little lumps of dough, and roll them to the size of a ping-pong ball.

5 Squash them

Place the balls on a baking sheet, leaving room for them to spread when they cook.

Press flat with a fork

Try using your thumb instead to press them down.

6 Bake them

Set the oven to 325°F (170°C). Bake for 15–20 min; cool on a rack.

1 Chocolate chips
2 tbsp

2 Cocoa powder
2 tbsp

3 Coconut
½ cup

4 Cinnamon
1 teaspoon

5 Candies
Press these into the cookies before you bake them.

Peanuts

6 Peanut butter
1 tablespoon

7 Raisins
⅓ cup

8 Almond extract
Add a few drops of almond extract and stick an almond on the top.

9 Sugar sprinkles
2 tbsp

10 Chopped nuts
½ cup

How to make 10 new cookies

Add your flavors in step 2.
If you want flavored cookies, then add your cocoa, chocolate chips, coconut, or cinnamon at stage 2 when your mixture is crumbly. Decorate your cookies with the nuts or candy just before you bake them.

Now get creative with your cookie cutters—see the next page.

create and bake

Bake me!

Make more of your cookie dough—roll it out, cut out some shapes, then have fun with icing.

cookie dough
See page 8

Makes about 24 cookies

1. Roll out the dough

Sprinkle flour on your work surface and a rolling pin. Now roll out your dough until it's ¼ in (5 mm) thick, then choose your cookie cutters and get shaping!

!

2. Ready to bake

Grease a baking sheet (see page 46) and place your shapes on it, leaving spaces between them.

Bake for 15 minutes

Preheat the oven to 325°F (170°C) **!**

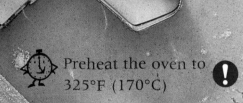

3. Cool off

Carefully remove the tray from the oven, let cookies cool a little on the tray, then transfer to a cooling rack.

Tip: If it is difficult to roll, cut the ball of dough in half, and roll out one half at a time.

Ice and sprinkle

Icing—Mix some powdered sugar and water with drops of food coloring.

Powdered sugar 3 tablespoons

water 3 teaspoons

Food coloring

Now add some sprinkles.

Icing mix

Put 3 tablespoons of powdered sugar in a bowl, add 3 teaspoons of water, and stir. Add more water if the icing is too thick.

Spoon the icing over the cookies and decorate them.

Adding color

Use a toothpick to add color to the icing mix. Keep adding and stirring until it's the color you want.

A fun-filled box of cookies

Make holes with the end of a straw. Do this before you bake the cookie.

Use a cocktail stick to make smaller features like eyes.

Cut out a shape, then use a smaller cutter to make a new shape.

Cherry pies

Fill buttery pastry pies

with sweet fillings and feed them to your sweetheart.

Canned cherry pie filling

Pastry
From page 14

+

Pie filling
8-oz (200-g) can

=

× 12 pies

Fruity pie fillings

When it's late summer, get out and pick your own fresh fruit. Soft fruits, such as blackberries, are perfect and go well with apples. Alternatively you can buy canned pie filling or try some of these other yummy ideas.

Makes 12 pies

Serve your pies with a dusting of powdered sugar and a spoonful of custard

All kinds of pies

Apple pie

Peel and chop some eating apples and put them into a saucepan with a little sugar and a couple of tablespoons of water. Boil them until they are soft, and when the mixture is cool, spoon it into pastry cases.

Mince pie

Just right for Christmas—a jar of mincemeat is packed full of candied fruit peel and raisins. Simply put it in the pastry case.

Lemon curd pie

For a tangy taste, buy a jar of lemon curd. Spoon it straight into the cases and pop on the lid.

Red berry jam pie

Sweet strawberry or raspberry jam makes a perfect partner for the plain pastry case.

Marmalade pie

For a rich, zesty taste, try using orange marmalade with thick-cut peel.

Rub in and roll out

The pies are made with shortcrust pastry—it's handy for all sorts of recipes, like sweet pies and tarts, and savories such as sausage rolls and quiche.

Butter
1 stick (½ cup)

+

All-purpose flour
2 cups

+

water
4–8 teaspoons

=

Pastry
Makes about 12 pies

Rub the butter and flour together

1

2 Add some water.

3 Squeeze into a ball.

Make some pies

Equipment

COOKIE CUTTERS
4 IN (10 CM)   2 IN (5 CM)

ROLLING PIN

KNIFE

BUN PAN AND PASTRY BRUSH

WIRE RACK

Make the leftovers into a ball and roll it out again.

Use the large cutter and press down firmly.

1 Roll out

Flour the surface and the rolling pin. Roll evenly over the pastry until it's about ¼ inch (5 mm) thick.

Don't press too hard. Add more flour if needed.

2 Make the pies

Gently place the pastry into the pan and fill the case with a spoonful or two of filling. Roll out more pastry and cut out the lids.

Roll out more pastry for the lid.

Gently rest the lid on top.

Don't overfill the cases, or they will overflow when cooked.

Use a straw to make a hole.

3 Ready to bake

Bake the pies. When they are ready, let them cool in the tray, then remove them and place on a rack.

Let them cool down before you take them out.

Leave to cool on a rack, then serve up.

Preheat the oven to 325°F (170°C)

Bake for 15 minutes

17

Tweetie pies

Crunchy Nuts and Seeds aren't just for birds—they make tasty nibbles to snack on anytime, even breakfast!

Tweetie Pies

Now go nuts!

Add one of these **or** why not add them all?

Sesame seeds

Raisins

Peanuts

Pumpkin seeds

Sunflower seeds

Try 2 tablespoons of each nut, seed, or fruit

Pine Nuts

Coconut

Chopped Nuts

 makes 18 pies

Mix up Some Pies

Crunchy pies—The longer you bake them, the crunchier they will get, and each bite will contain a completely different crunch!

 Preheat the oven to 375°F (190°C).

TWEETY PIE TOOLS

MIXING BOWL

WOODEN SPOON

KNIFE

TABLESPOON

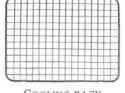
PASTRY BRUSH

BUN PAN

COOLING RACK

20

Mix the butter and sugar together with a wooden spoon until the mixture is creamy.

Butter

Sugar

1 Cream together

Give it a stir.

2 Pour in the oats

Spoon up some mixture and roll it into a ball.

5 make the pies

Grease the pan, then put in the balls of mixture.

6 Press them down

Then give it another stir.

3 Pour in the Honey

Add as many as you like and stir them in.

4 Go Nuts!

 Bake in the oven for 10 to 15 minutes.

7 Into the oven !

Use a knife to lift them out of the pan.

They will keep in an airtight jar for two to three weeks.

8 Leave to cool

Come for tea!

Fruit
Any dried fruit can be used. These are raisin scones spread with butter.

Sweet
Try these sweet scones with jam and cream.

Cheesy
These savory scones are topped with grated cheese for an even tastier treat.

It's tea time!

Scones for tea—invite your friends over for sweet and savory treats.

Butter
3 tbsp

+

Plain flour
1¾ cups

+

Milk
½ cup

=

1 plain scone

☺ Makes 8 slices

Clever scones

Use this plain scone mixture to create new recipes. Just add all sorts of ingredients, from sugar, dried fruit, and seeds to olives and cheese. Make a meal of them!

More tea, Owl?
Have a scone, too.

Butter Flour

Rub the butter and flour together to make crumbs (see page 46).

1 Rub together

Add the sugar __OR__ fruit __OR__ cheese at this stage.

Mix in the flavoring.

2 Add the flavoring

3 Pour in the milk

Scones x 3

Make sweet or savory—Follow the steps the same way for all the recipes. But at Step 2, choose the flavor you want and mix it in. Then bake and enjoy them fresh from the oven.

EQUIPMENT

MIXING BOWL   BAKING SHEET   COOLING RACK
PASTRY BRUSH   KNIFE

Plain Sweet

2 tbsp superfine sugar

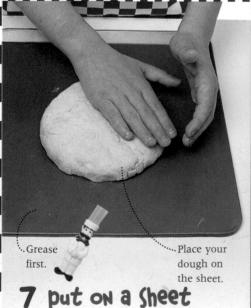

Grease first.

Place your dough on the sheet.

7 Put on a sheet

Divide the dough up— 8 pieces works best.

8 Cut into sections

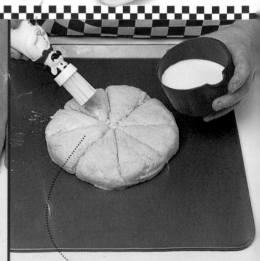

Brush with milk for a glossy finish.

9 Get ready to bake

Use a knife to stir the mixture...

4 Stir with a knife

Bring all of the mixture together.

5 Make a ball

Flour a clean surface.

Flatten the ball to about 1 in (3 cm) thick...

Don't handle the dough too much.

6 Flour and flatten

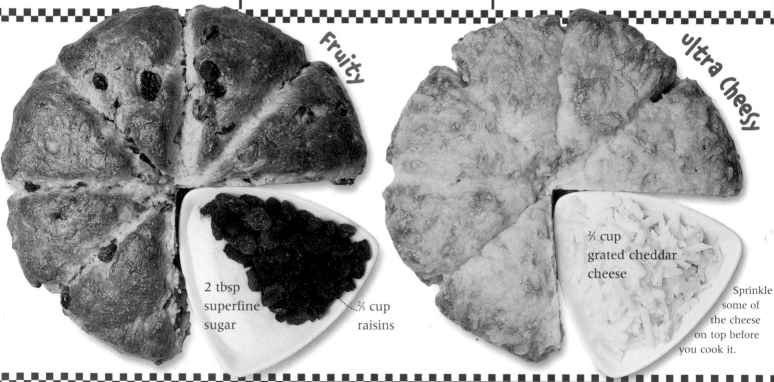

Fruity

2 tbsp superfine sugar

⅔ cup raisins

Ultra Cheesy

⅔ cup grated cheddar cheese

Sprinkle some of the cheese on top before you cook it.

❗ Preheat the oven to 425°F (220°C).

Bake for 25 minutes, take out of the oven, and cool on a rack.

Scone tip

Eat it on the same day as you bake it.

I like to eat it fresh from the oven.

10 All done

monkey bread

Bakes like a cake

and slices like bread. Monkey enjoys a piece for dessert or a snack in his lunchbox. *You'll go bananas over my yummy recipe!*

EQUIPMENT

BOWL   LOAF PAN   COOLING RACK   PASTRY BRUSH   FORK   SPOON   WOODEN SPOON

Rub the butter and flour together until they are like bread crumbs (see page 46).

1 Rubbing in

Add in sugar and raisins and give it a stir.

2 Add Sugar and raisins

Beat the eggs, spoon in the honey, and stir them in.

3 Add eggs and honey

In a small bowl, mash the bananas with a fork.

4 Mash the bananas

5 Add the bananas

6 Give it a Stir

Dip the brush in oil and brush over the pan.

7 Grease the pan

Set the oven to 350°F (180°C). Bake for 1 hour.

8 Pour it in

Is it done? Turn to page 46 to find out how to test it.

9 Leave to cool

Turn out your bread

Slide the knife between the cake and the pan.

10 Slide around a knife

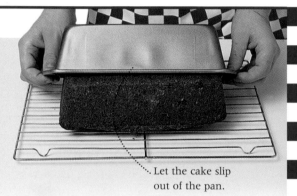

Let the cake slip out of the pan.

11 Flip over the pan

The cake will cut more easily when it's cold.

12 Nearly ready to eat!

Slice up the bread and serve it up

I like mine spread with butter

MiNi MoNKeY MuffiNs

To make these **yummy** muffins, use the same mixture as the monkey bread but fill a muffin pan instead.

Makes 12 mini breads

MUFFIN PAN AND PAPER CASES

Just use your monkey bread mixture

Try these bread variations
instead of bananas...
apple and cinnamon

2 apples peeled and chopped....

....1/2 cup milk

1 teaspoon cinnamon

BuNNy bites

Grated peel and juice of an orange

2 carrots peeled and grated

1 teaspoon mixed spice

As in step 5 on the previous page.

Preheat the oven to 350°F (180°C)

1 Stir it up

Carefully spoon in the mixture.

2 Fill up the cases

Bake them for 15 minutes.

3 Bake your breads

making variations

To make the variations, go back to Step 5 of monkey bread, then, instead of adding the banana, put in the ingredients for apple or carrot breads and mix it all up in the same way.

Storage

Eat them warm or keep them fresh in an airtight jar. They'll keep for about two weeks.

Carrot bunny bites

Apple and cinnamon

Mini Monkey Muffins

Chocolate chunk cookies

Forget Store-bought

cookies, these are much tastier!
Use a good-quality chocolate
chopped up into big chunks.

☺ Makes 12 cookies

You will need . . .

Soft brown Sugar
⅓ cup

Superfine Sugar
⅓ cup

Butter
1 stick (½ cup)

1 Egg

All-purpose flour
1½ cups

Baking Soda
1 teaspoon

Chocolate chunks
7 oz (175 g)

EQUIPMENT

MIXING BOWL

SPOON

KNIFE

WOODEN SPOON

BAKING SHEET

PASTRY BRUSH

COOLING RACK

Butter

Brown and superfine Sugar

Soft butter is easier to mix with the sugar.

1 Start creaming

See page 47 to beat an egg.

Preheat the oven to 375°F (190°C)

2 Add beaten egg

Mix in the flour.

3 Stir in the flour

Get help chopping the chunks.

4 Add chocolate

Spoon four blobs on each sheet.

5 Spoon onto sheet

Bake for 10–12 minutes, then take out of the oven and cool on a rack.

6 Bake them

Prepare the sheet for the next batch of cookies.

Let them cool before moving to a rack.

7 Cooling down

Eat them when they are still warm

Chocolate tip
Stick chunks of chocolate on top of the dough blobs before cooking.

Happy birthday, Bear!
Let's have a party.
we can ask Owl to come.

Yes please!

Bake a cake

...and celebrate with this chocolate-covered treat. Share it with your special friends when you have a reason to say... "Let's have a party!"

Mmm... chocolate

Makes 8–12 slices

How's your cake, Little Ted?

33

All-in-one mix

Simply beat all the ingredients together in the bowl.

This recipe makes a plain sponge cake. Baking two cakes means you can layer them with jam or fresh cream. You can also add flavorings to the mixture, like cocoa powder, dried fruit, or vanilla.

Baking powder
1 teaspoon

Flour
1 cup
self-rising

Eggs
2 large

Butter
1 stick (½ cup)
softened

Sugar
⅔ cup
superfine

Bake a cake

Sponge cake

Divide the mixture evenly between two lined pans (see page 47). Spread the mixture flat so the cake rises evenly. Let them cool down before you spread on the frosting. Keep the cake in a cool place and eat within two days.

 Preheat the oven to 325°F (170°C)

Top and fill

Chocolate cream

Use good-quality chocolate mixed with heavy cream. Melt the chocolate first, then spoon in the cream.

Chocolate
7 oz (200 g)

Heavy cream
6 tablespoons

Prepare the pans (see page 47).

Share the mixture between the pans.

1 Fill the pans

Spread the mixture out to the sides evenly.

Bake in the oven for 20 minutes.

2 Spread the mixture

Stir the chunks around to help them melt.

Watch out— HOT water

1 Melt the chocolate

Take the bowl away from the hot water.

Stir the cream into the melted chocolate.

2 Add the cream

make the mixture

Put all the ingredients into a bowl and mix together for two minutes. Keep the mixer on a low setting.

EQUIPMENT

MIXING BOWL

ELECTRIC MIXER

KNIFE

SPOON

WIRE RACK

2 CAKE PANS 8 IN (20 CM)

PASTRY BRUSH

PARCHMENT PAPER

Very hot water—don't overfill the bowl.

chocolate

To melt the chocolate, pour very hot water into a bowl. Set another bowl on top and put the chocolate in. The heat from the water will melt it.

Break the chocolate into chunks first.

Watch out— HOT water

Run a knife around the edge where the cake may stick to the pan.

Allow the cakes to cool down.

3 Out of the oven

Hold the rim of the pan.

Give it a bit of a tap.

Tip the cake out of the pan.

4 Remove the cakes

Carefully peel back the paper.

The cakes should be cold before the adding the frosting.

5 Leave to cool

Place the top layer on

Put two spoonfuls on the bottom layer.

Spread it with a knife.

3 Spread the filling

Spoon on the rest of the mixture.

4 Pour on the frosting

Use a knife to spread the mixture over the top and down the sides.

5 Spread it all over

35

meringue mountain

whisk up egg whites into sweet
frothy peaks to make delicious desserts.

Egg whites
2 whites

Superfine sugar
⅔ cup

Makes about
12 small peaks

See page 48 for how
to separate an egg.

Fruity nest

Spoon whipped cream onto a nest and top it off with pieces of fruit.

Peak sandwich

Sandwich two meringue peaks together with whipped cream.

Mmmmeringue

Meringues are made from egg whites mixed with sugar baked in a very cool oven until they are crunchy on the outside and soft inside—mmmm!

Serve up your meringues with cream and fruit, or just plain and simple.

It's ready when you can turn the bowl upside-down over your head without the egg whites sliding.

Use a big, clean bowl.

See page 48 for how to separate the egg whites.

Use the mixer at top speed.

3 is it ready?

1 whisk the egg whites

2 Keep whisking

whisk up a mountain

whisking is fun—An electric mixer makes the egg white froth up quicker than by hand, but remember to let it stop spinning before you take it out of the bowl, or you'll cover the kitchen!

Meringue hints and tips

• Whisk the egg whites just enough—try the "over the head" test as in step 3.
• Add the sugar a tablespoon at a time while whisking. Keep repeating this until all the sugar is used up.
• Grease the tray first to stop the paper from slipping.

Grease the tray, then cover with parchment paper.

Preheat the oven to 275°F (140°C)

7 Spoon out some peaks

Pour in the sugar—about a tablespoon at a time.

4 Add some sugar and whisk

Whisk in the sugar BUT not at full speed.

5 Keep whisking

See page 46 for whisking tips.

When all the sugar is in, give the mixture a final whisk.

The mixture should look glossy and stand up in peaks.

6 Now it's peaky

EQUIPMENT

MIXING BOWL

ELECTRIC MIXER

TEASPOON AND TABLESPOON

PARCHMENT PAPER

BAKING SHEET

PASTRY BRUSH

Press the peak down with a spoon to make a nest.

Make a snowman with peaks joined together.

Bake in the oven for 2 hours.

8 Ready to bake

Take the meringues out of the oven.

Leave them for a few hours to dry out.

9 All dried out

yummy bread

Make bread taste more interesting by using grainy flour and sprinkles of seeds inside and out. This yummy bread is fun to bake and eat.

You will need:

Butter
1½ tbsp)

Grainy flour
1¾ cups
Multi-grain
bread flour

And a beaten egg
for a glossy finish

white flour
1¾ cups
white
bread flour

yeast
1 packet
fast-acting yeast

Sugar and salt
1 teaspoon
brown sugar,
1 teaspoon Salt

water
1¼ cups
warm water

Makes 12
rolls

Extra seeds on top. As well as adding some seeds to your bread mixture, sprinkle a few on top—not just for decoration, but because they make the bread taste good, too!

You will need lots of different seeds

Sesame seeds

Poppy seeds

Sunflower seeds

Pumpkin seeds

41

Make a well to pour the water in.

Mix it with a wooden spoon.

Put the flour, yeast, sugar, and salt in a bowl and rub in the butter.

Add some seeds now if you want to.

Make it a ball with your hands.

1 Rub together

2 Add water

3 Mix it up

How to make bread

Bread flour—It's important to use special bread flour for baking bread. It comes in white, whole-wheat, and multi-grain, and for this recipe it has malt grains in it. too.

Bread tips

Yeast likes warmth to help it grow, and this will help your bread to rise.

• If all the things you work with are warm, such as the bowl and the room, this will help.

• Make sure the water isn't too hot or it will kill the yeast and your bread won't rise.

A beaten egg

Grease the sheet.

Place the dough balls on the sheet.

Cover with plastic wrap and leave in a warm place for about 40 minutes.

When they have doubled in size, they are ready to decorate.

Brush them with beaten egg.

7 Prepare the Sheet

8 The rolls have grown!

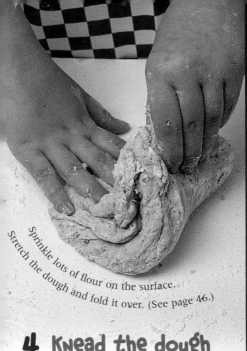

Sprinkle lots of flour on the surface.
Stretch the dough and fold it over. (See page 46.)

4 Knead the dough

Press your knuckles into the dough.
Add more flour if needed.
Repeat steps 4 and 5 for 6 minutes.

5 Keep kneading

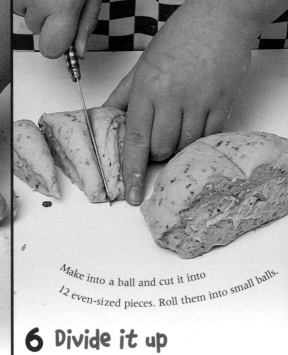

Make into a ball and cut it into
12 even-sized pieces. Roll them into small balls.

6 Divide it up

Preheat the oven to
425°F (220°C)

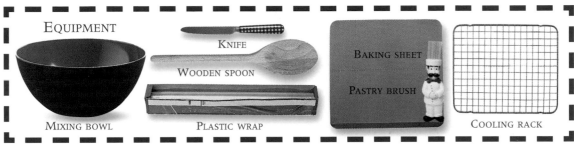

EQUIPMENT

KNIFE

WOODEN SPOON

BAKING SHEET

PASTRY BRUSH

COOLING RACK

MIXING BOWL

PLASTIC WRAP

Now sprinkle
on the seeds.

Bake for 20 to 25
minutes, then take
out of the oven and
cool on a rack.

9 Get ready to bake

Serve up your rolls
fresh from the oven
with you favorite filling

Mold your dough

Now it's time to play with your dough. Make a dough ball as shown before, but before you bake it, try molding it into different shapes.

Cooking the shapes

Follow the steps as for yummy bread, put your shapes on a greased pan, cover them, and allow them to rise until they double in size. Then bake for 25 minutes.

Braided bread

1 Roll your dough into three sausage shapes.

2 Squeeze your dough together at one end.

Dough balls

Roll into a sausage shape, then cut and roll into dough balls.

or a Pizza

1 Flatten a dough ball.

Grated cheese

Chopped olives

Spread a tablespoon of tomato paste on first.

Then a tablespoon of chopped canned tomatoes.

2 Add some toppings, then bake in the oven.

Dough boy

Make small balls of dough and stick them to your rolls to make faces.

3 Bring one sausage over to the middle.

Repeat on the other side.

Finish braiding, squash the ends together, and place on the tray.

Bake all kinds of yummy fun

Bread tastes best when it's warm from the oven.

Try baked dough balls with garlic butter.

Garlic butter

45

you can bake

Baking Methods

Baking recipes use different methods to mix the same ingredients to achieve different results. Whether it's cookies, cakes, or pastry, this book uses a few of the basic methods. Here they are with explanations of what they do.

Rubbing in

Using your thumb and fingertips, rub the butter and flour together until the mixture looks like bread crumbs. This is used for a lot of the recipes in this book, such as pastry and cookies.

Creaming

This is when you mix or beat the butter and sugar together with a wooden spoon so that they make a creamy mixture. In this book, it's used to start the chunky chocolate cookies.

Dough

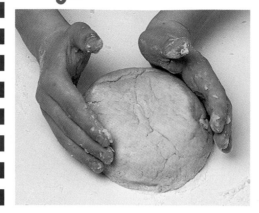

Dough is a name given to the mixture that makes pastry, cookies, scones, or bread, but they behave differently when cooked. Bread dough needs kneading because it has yeast in it. Other dough should be handled lightly.

Tips

Let your dough rest in the refrigerator for half an hour before using it.

To store your dough, wrap it in plastic and put in the refrigerator.

Cookie and pastry dough

Kneading

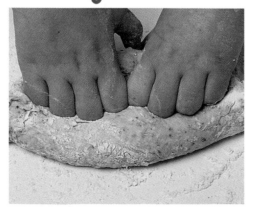

This is what you do to bread dough to get the yeast working: Fold the dough over itself and press your knuckles into it. Repeat this over and over again. Then leave it in a warm place to rise.

Whisking

Whisking egg whites can be done with a hand whisk, but an electric mixer is much faster. Don't let any egg yolk get in or it won't work. Whisk at full speed until the mixture stands up in peaks.

Is it done?

To check if the monkey bread is cooked, put a fork in the center of it when it's due to come out of the oven. If the fork comes out with some mixture on it, it's not cooked, so put it back in the oven.

To keep your cookies, cakes, and tweety pies fresh, store them in an AIRTIGHT jar or tin and they will keep for a week or two.

Greasing baking pans

This will help to stop your baked goods from sticking as they cook.

Put a little oil onto a pastry brush and sweep it all over the pan.

Oil

Line a pan with paper

To make sure your cakes have no chance of sticking, line the pan parchment paper. Brush the pan with oil first so that the paper sticks to it.

Hang the paper over the sides.

Use the paper to pull the cake out of the pan when the cake is cooked.

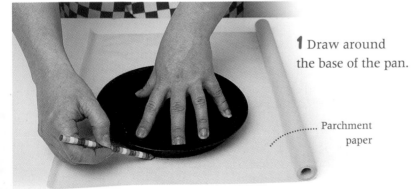

1 Draw around the base of the pan.

Parchment paper

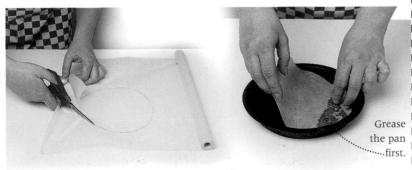

2 Cut out the shape.

3 Place the paper in the pan.

Grease the pan first.

Cracking an egg

How to get an egg out of the shell.

The secret is to be firm and gentle at the same time.

tap tap

1 Tap the egg firmly against the edge of a bowl.

2 Gently press your thumbs into the crack.

3 Pull the two shells apart and let the egg fall out.

white

yellow yolk

Beating an egg

Mixing the egg white and yolk together.

It's best to beat an egg before adding it to a recipe.

Use a fork to mix.

Move it quickly in a circular action.

Separate an egg— the easy way

Sometimes you will only want the egg white or the yolk. So you need to separate them carefully. It takes a bit of practice, so have some spare eggs in case you break the yolk.

1

Break an egg into a bowl.

Egg cup

Small, clean bowl

2

Cover the yolk with an egg cup.

Push the egg cup down.

3

Hold the egg cup down very firmly and tip the bowl.

Let the white fall into another bowl.

Meringue tip

Don't get any egg yolk in the egg white or your meringues won't work.

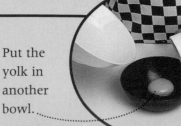

Put the yolk in another bowl.

Acknowledgments

With thanks to...
Billy Bull, James Bull, Seriya Ezigwe, Daniel Ceccarelli, Harry Holmstoel for being avid chefs.

All images © Dorling Kindersley.
For further information, see:
www.dkimages.com